LIFE SKILLS SERIES

Increasing
PEACE

STEPHEN MATTHEW

RIVER

PUBLISHING

River Publishing & Media Ltd

info@river-publishing.co.uk

British Library Cataloguing in Publication Data

A catalogue record for this book is available from the British Library

ISBN 978-1-908393-81-4

Contents

The Life Skills Series
Equipping you to live an abundant life

Jesus said: *'I have come that they may have life, and have it to the full' (John 10:10).*

God's will is for every Christian to enjoy an abundant life on earth followed by an eternal life in heaven. It should just get better and better! Living it to the full takes skill and application.

In this series of Bible studies, we explore some of the Christian life skills that will equip you to live the abundant life Jesus has given you to the full. The truths examined and principles discussed are simply tools that must be put to use. The more you use them, the more skilled you will become at living the abundant Christian life you know God has for you.

These studies are deliberately packed with God's Word. Most scriptures are written out in full as part of the text, so reading each lesson takes you on a Bible study through the subject. I have presented the material in this way because above all else, you need to know what God says about these subjects. It is then your responsibility to apply his Word and ways into your personal situation.

Abundant Life Skills are ideal for individual or group study. There's also plenty of space for you to make your own notes as you read and think things through.

These studies will equip you with skills for abundant living and we are confident that as you apply them they will make a lasting impact on you, your friends, family, church and the wider community.

Stephen Matthew

Other titles in this series by Stephen Matthew:

- Battle for the MIND

- MONEY Matters

- Bringing the BIBLE to Life

For more information visit:
www.stephenmatthew.com

Chapter 1
Peace

Everybody wants peace.

Peace is awesome! It is the condition in which we all prefer to do life. Peace is all pervading yet sometimes hard to define or explain. Peace is a feeling, an experience, a state, an essential condition the human soul longs for.

Peace is therefore pursued; we crave a life of peace and we want it in increasing measure. 'If only I had peace!' is the cry of every human heart.

The good news is that true peace can be yours. Not the temporary fleeting kind but the lasting kind. In this short book we will be exploring this reality and equipping you to experience it to the full. Our aim is to live in the fullness of God's promise that *'the peace of God, which transcends all understanding, will guard your hearts and your minds in Christ Jesus' (Philippians 4:7).*

The essence of peace

How would you define peace?

Peace has many expressions and applications. We use phrases like 'peace of mind', having 'peace in our heart' or 'relational peace'. Then there is the peace we say we feel about a decision we have made, and of course the big one: world peace! What's more, we often use peace as a relative term rather than an absolute one. So, 'I am more at peace than I was'. Even of war zones it is frequently reported that a region is enjoying a time of 'relative peace'. So it is enjoying peace but not complete peace … or something!

For this reason, dictionaries usually carry a number of definitions of the word 'peace'. They typically include:

Personal peace: which can be defined as 'the state of being calm or quiet' (Oxford English Dictionary). Some zoom in a bit closer to the inner nature of personal peace and define it as 'a state of mental calm and serenity, with no anxiety' (Encarta World English Dictionary).

Relational peace: is defined as 'the state of living in friendship with somebody without arguing' (Oxford). This is clear and simple. Some fill it out further adding phrases like 'freedom from conflict or disagreement among people or groups of people' (Encarta).

Political peace: which can be defined as 'freedom from war' (Oxford) or 'a situation or a period of time in which there is no war or violence in a country or an area' (Encarta).

The Bible encourages us to seek all three of these expressions of peace. We are promised **personal peace** as we steadfastly trust in God (Isaiah 26:3), urged to pursue **relational peace** by ensuring that *'as far as it depends on you, live at peace with everyone (Romans 12:18)'*, and we are to pray *'for kings and all those in authority, that we may live peaceful and quiet lives' (1 Timothy 2:2)*, which is **political peace.**

However, it is clear that all expressions of peace have a common root. Relational peace and political peace flow out of lives that are themselves in personal peace. So that must be our starting point.

True peace, its essence and essential nature, must first be embraced as a deep personal experience; an inner knowing that all is well; a tranquillity, serenity and calmness that fills your heart and mind. This is your felt, personal experience of peace. From within you it then flows out, influencing and pervading all you do.

The road to peace

Everyone starts their journey to personal peace from a negative perspective. They simply feel the lack of it. Life confronts them with uncertainties about themselves, other people and the world around them. This leads to worry, anxiety and stress, all of which go on inside their mind and heart, eating away at their ability to relax, sleep and rest in peace.

What's on the inside of people always comes out – as Jesus said, *'out of the overflow of the heart the mouth speaks' (Matthew 12:36).* Words and actions rooted in fear, anxiety and unrest flow from their lives, often resulting in relational disharmony, mistrust of other people and a whole range of human conflicts. From these personal and relational experiences of dis-peace everyone starts their journey towards true peace.

Then, from time to time, they get a glimpse of what they are seeking. A relational conflict resolved leads to a good feeling … but then it passes. A great personal decision leads to a good nights sleep … but then they wake up! They meet other people who seem to be essentially calm; who have a certain quality they admire, a peacefulness which is good to be around … but how on earth is it obtained? Lasting personal peace remains elusive, so the journey goes on.

Some seek peace in isolation and solitude, only to find that even there, inner disquiet remains unresolved. Others simply drown out the pain of their dis-peace with a fast-paced life, administering adrenaline inducing short-term fixes of every imaginable kind. The road to peace takes some to religion and spirituality, while it takes others to a place of a denying they need them at all.

The one thing every traveller on the road to peace agrees with is that something is missing. They need peace, or whatever it is, that will remove the negative effects of the lack of peace they are experiencing in their lives.

For most reading this book, the road will have taken them to God, or at least to an openness to consider that their answer may be linked to the one their Christian family or friends call God.

God's perspective

The Bible teaches us that every human being is born in dis-peace. The way it describes the dis-peace is to say we are all born in sin. David expressed it this way:

> 'Surely I was sinful at birth, sinful from the time my mother conceived me (Psalm 51:5).'

Sin is the condition that separates people from God – so there is animosity between us and God from the moment we are born, which is dis-peace. It is inherent, part of our nature, and it is our felt need to fix that breach of relationship with God and find that elusive personal peace, which sets us on a journey that eventually leads us to God.

Christians believe that personal peace is only found when the inner dis-peace we are born with is resolved. So, how does that happen?

Peace is only found when you are personally reconciled to God, the one who created you and gave you life. The search for peace is about fixing that broken relationship we are born into. Sadly, we cannot fix it ourselves – sin is just too big a problem. But the good news is that God fixed it for us! He did this be sending Jesus to act on behalf of every human being. He came into this world as a sinless baby and then chose to take all the sin we were born with on himself. By dying on the Cross he paid the penalty for that sin once and for all, that is, he dealt with all the consequences of us being sinners – including the dis-peace we inherited. So now, everyone who believes Jesus did that for them is what the Bible describes as 'saved', 'born again', has a brand new start because they are reconciled to God. This is how Paul describes it:

'Therefore, if anyone is in Christ, he is a new creation; the old has gone, the new has come! All this is from God, who reconciled us to himself through Christ ... God was reconciling the world to himself in Christ, not counting men's sins against them... We implore you on Christ's behalf: Be reconciled to God. God made him who had no sin to be sin for us, so that in him we might become the righteousness of God' (2 Corinthians 5:17-21).

Salvation is peace

To be a Christian – saved, born again, converted, have a brand new start ... or whatever you prefer to call it – is to have peace. The terms are synonymous. You may say 'I found Christ' but you could equally say 'I found peace'. Look at the following scriptures and you will see what I mean:

Describing Jesus' death on the Cross Isaiah says:

*'He was pierced for our transgressions, he was crushed for our iniquities; **the punishment that brought us peace was upon him**, and by his wounds we are healed' (Isaiah 53:5).*

When prophesying about what Jesus was coming to do, Zechariah the father of John the Baptist declared he was coming:

'To shine on those living in darkness and in the shadow of death, **to guide our feet into the path of peace***' (Luke 1:79).*

Just before the crucifixion, anticipating he would be rejected by the Jews, Jesus looked at the people of Jerusalem and wept saying:

'If you, even you, had only known on this day what would bring you **peace***' (Luke 19:42).*

Then, as the church grew and the Gospel was preached, Peter described it as being:

'The good news of **peace through Jesus Christ***, who is Lord of all' (Acts 10:36).*

But maybe Paul put it best of all. To the Christians in Ephesus he wrote:

'For **he himself is our peace***, who has made the two one and has destroyed the barrier, the dividing wall of hostility … thus making peace … He came and preached peace to you who were far away and peace to those who were near (Ephesians 2:14-17).*

And to the Roman Christians he said:

'Therefore, since we have been justified through faith, **we have peace with God through our Lord Jesus Christ** *(Romans 5:1)*

Coming to Jesus and making him the Lord of your life is therefore to find peace. We have peace because we are in relationship with the one who is in himself peace, Jesus, the one the Old Testament prophets describe as being the *'Prince of Peace'* (Isaiah 9:6).

So, true personal peace is only ever found when people find Jesus, the 'Prince of Peace'.

Peace fruit

Once the root of our personal dis-peace is dealt with, the fruit will soon be seen. Now that Christ lives in us by the Holy Spirit, the fruit of the Holy Spirit can be produced, which includes peace:

'The fruit of the Spirit is love, joy, **peace**, *patience, kindness, goodness, faithfulness, gentleness and self-control' (Galatians 5:22).*

First, peace with God results in us being more at peace with **ourselves**. We no longer need to strive to be something we are not, or to fix the dis-peace by having material things or attaining any human target or achievement. We become more at peace with our unique individuality, personality and the aptitudes God has given us. We simply rest in all that Christ has made us and done for us.

This process begins within us, in our mind and heart, at the centre of our being. Our inner condition at that core level shapes everything we subsequently say and do; it is the seat of our reasoning. Paul puts it like this:

'*The mind of sinful man is death, but* **the mind controlled by the Spirit is life and peace**' *(Romans 8:6).*

This inner condition of being at peace with God, and increasingly with ourselves, also gives us the basis of **relational peace**; that is, we increasingly relate to other people in a godly way that is characterised by peace, something we will explore in more detail later in this book.

So, only in Christ do we find the basis of lasting:

- peace with GOD
- peace with OURSELVES
- peace with OTHERS

Your peace

Jesus is the source and essence of peace according to the Bible. Millions of Christians have discovered this to be true and are living a life characterised by the peace that only God can give. I pray that you have found that peace. If not, you can discover it today by placing your trust in God and believing he has made a way through Jesus to exchange your dis-peace for his amazing 'peace that passes understanding'.

Your personal peace depends on believing this, so talk to a Christian friend about how they became a Christian, go and visit a Church near you and enquire about how you can get to know Jesus, the Prince of Peace.

For everyone reading this who already knows Jesus and has tasted the peace only he can give – the rest of this book is for you. We are going on a journey into peace. We will explore its dynamics together and, best of all, learn how to genuinely live in increasing peace.

Chapter 2
The Price of Peace

Felt peace

Having established that peace is synonymous with salvation for the Christian, we need to tackle a very practical question: If Christians have peace in Christ, why don't they always feel it? Why is peace sometimes so elusive?

The truth is, as Christians we sometimes emanate stress, worry, uncertainty, doubt or fear. All of which are the opposite of peace. In fact some Christians are total stress-heads!

Over the years in my role as a Pastor I have had to assist believers who were worried about not being in God's will, others live in fear that the devil is out to get them, some go through periods of doubt about their eternal salvation and for many it is simply learning to handle the stresses and strains of modern life, like paying their bills, coping at work and handling family relationships. It can be a myriad of things but they all have in common that the person is not in peace. Why is this, when they are soundly saved and spirit filled believers? They have peace but it is not their felt experience.

The answer lies in understanding that peace does not exist in a vacuum; it is inextricably linked to the wider context of your life. Peace has roots, a clear source, and if that root is disturbed, cut or ignored, peace can be lost.

If you 'just want peace' in your life today, you must examine that root and get to grips with what God has to say about the pre-condition for peace in every area of your life. Once that is understood, we can explore how to increase peace in each area of our lives. The result is an ability to live in 'felt peace' and not just conceptual or positional peace, which you know you have by virtue of being a Christian.

The root of peace

First, think back to when you first got true peace – the moment of your salvation. What happened at that point?

Scripture describes the process of salvation as follows:

> 'If you confess with your mouth, "Jesus is Lord," and believe in your heart that God raised him from the dead, you will be saved' (Romans 10:9).

So, peace came the moment you made Jesus Lord; when you gave him control of your life, thus making him the Boss, the King, the Commander. It was at that point you entered the Kingdom of God, which is the sphere of his rule. From that point on you determined to do things the King's way. Like all Christians, you felt his wonderful peace for the first time and that peace increased as you deliberately did things God's way.

Therefore, we can establish that *peace is linked to the rule of God in your life*. When you do things the King's way, you feel peace. The King's way is the right way and this is the essence of living in God's Kingdom.

Notice how Paul describes the Kingdom of God:

> 'The kingdom of God is ... righteousness, peace and joy in the Holy Spirit' (Romans 14:17).

The Kingdom of God exists where people are consciously living under God's rule, which means living in righteousness or doing things God's 'right' way.

That righteousness cannot be earned or bought, it is a gift from God. As sinners we are unable to do enough 'right' to make us holy enough to live in relationship with God in his Kingdom. But by faith in Christ's sacrifice for our sin, we can receive this wonderful gift of righteousness:

> 'God made him who had no sin to be sin for us, so that in him we might become the righteousness of God' (2 Corinthians 5:21).

Jesus took our sin and gave us his righteousness – this is the great exchange at the core of salvation. Believing this by faith is what saves us or makes us righteous. And because we are now right with God we feel peace with God, because peace flows from righteousness. So it is our actual felt experience that entering the Kingdom of God is a 'matter of righteousness, peace and joy' – in that order.

My point is this: **Peace comes from doing right.** It is the fruit of righteousness, which we initially receive at salvation. We were formerly sinners, or wicked, and the Bible says *'There is no peace for the wicked' (Isaiah 57:21).* But now in Christ we are righteous and therefore have peace. That's amazing!

Government and peace

This connection between righteousness and peace is seen throughout the Bible – it is simply the way God works with us. For example when Jesus was teaching his followers not to worry, which is felt dis-peace, he taught them to:

> 'Seek first his kingdom and his righteousness, and all these things will be given to you' (Matthew 6:33).

Therefore, seeking how to do things God's right way is the antidote to worry! Righteousness leads to peace. In the Old Testament Isaiah puts it superbly when he says:

> 'The fruit of righteousness will be peace; the effect of righteousness will be quietness and confidence forever' (Isaiah 32:17).

So, peace is clearly linked to righteousness, which is the first quality of God's Kingdom. To enjoy *increasing peace,* the title of this study, you must therefore increasingly do things God's right way in your life – his Kingdom rule must increase.

This is exactly how Isaiah said Jesus would operate. He prophesied:

*'For to us a child is born, to us a son is given, and the **government** will be on his shoulders. And he will be called … **Prince of Peace**. Of the **increase of his government and peace** there will be no end' (Isaiah 9:6-7).*

Where Jesus rules, there is peace. Where his government or rule increases, so does peace. This leads us to two clear conclusions:

To seek peace without seeking God's government in your life is a fruitless exercise.

To experience *increasing peace* we must first actively implement the *increasing government* of God in our lives.

How? By increasingly doing things God's way. From our perspective, that is the price of peace.

Paying the price for peace

Let's explore a few practical examples of this principle. Remember we are talking here about people who are already Christians – they have true peace in Christ – but are experiencing felt dis-peace in certain aspects of their daily lives. They want the felt dis-peace to be removed by the 'increasing peace' they have in their fundamental relationship with God. They want increasing peace, which first requires an increase of God's government.

a. Dis-peace in Finances

We have all worried about money at one time or other. But the dis-peace such worry brings can be a heavy burden to bear. It eats away at our soul, keeping us awake at night and draining us emotionally. How can we find increasing financial peace in these situations? Only by increasingly handling our money God's way – by increasing his government.

God has a very clear view of how we should handle money and material wealth, which is the subject of *Money Matters*, another practical title in this series that you will find very helpful if you want to understand the full picture of God's attitude to your financial affairs.

Increasing financial peace requires us to increasingly apply God's principles of money management in our lives. Things like:

- Having God's attitude to money rather than this world's.

- Acknowledging God as our source and provider, which is at the heart of putting him first in our giving and the principle of tithing.

- Worshiping the provider, not the provision: it is the *'love of money' (1 Timothy 6:10)* that is at the root of many evils.

- Believing that fundamentally all our money is his; we just have the use of it to invest and manage for the Master; we are stewards not owners.

- Handling money righteously; earning it and paying our way.

- Managing our money wisely with godly shrewdness and getting all the best deals.

- Having a giving ethic, living to give rather than to get because *'it is more blessed to give than receive' (Acts 20:35)*.

Ultimately, money is to be our servant not our master.

If you will increasingly develop the financial principles of God's government, you will increasingly enjoy financial peace. Worrying about money will become a thing of the past and a delightful contentment with what you have will develop. You will enjoy genuine prosperity, which is having enough to live on whilst also having enough left over to share with others (2 Corinthians 9:10-11).

Are you willing to manage your money God's way? Doing so is the price of your financial peace.

b. Dis-peace at work

Dis-peace in your work world requires an increase of God's government in your work ethic, attitudes and practices.

God has a very clear view of how we should work which, again, is beyond the scope of this short lesson to explore in detail. But working as someone living under God's rule – as a child of his kingdom – requires us to work:

- As if Jesus was our boss (Colossians 3:23, Ephesians 6:5).

- Working just as diligently when we are working alone as when we are being watched (Colossians 3:22).

- Conducting ourselves in a way that gives the unsaved a positive view of Christianity (Matthew 5:16).

- Treating your boss with due respect (Ephesians 6:5).

- And if you are a boss, treating your employees well (Ephesians 6:9).

- Regarding our work as a gift from God (Ecclesiastes 5:19).

- And always relating to work colleagues in a godly way.

If you will increasingly develop these principles of God's government, you will enjoy increasing peace in your work. That is the price of peace at work.

c. Dis-peace at home

The people we love the most sometimes cause us the most dis-peace! Just living in the same house together creates the opportunity for a whole range of interpersonal conflicts, tensions and unrest. But as I hope you are beginning to understand, any dis-peace can be soothed and removed by a willingness to increase God's government in our family relationships. For example:

- God has clear principles for **husbands and wives** to live by. They include:

- Loving each other like Christ loves the Church (Ephesians 5:24-25).

- Submitting to one another out of mutual respect for the differences they each bring to the relationship.

- Speaking the truth in love (Ephesians 4:15) and not letting sun go down on your anger! (Ephesians 4:26).

Similarly, God has principles for *parents and children* to live by:

- Children are to obey their parents until they reach adulthood, they can then make their own choices having been shown how to do so. But they must always have an attitude of honour. (Exodus 20:12, Ephesians 6:1)

- Parents are not to exasperate their children (Ephesians 6:4).

- Yet parents have to discipline and train their children in a loving environment with clear boundaries (Proverbs 22:6).

Where children have no boundaries, chaos results. Where they have clear boundaries to live within, they thrive.

Neither of the family related lists above are exhaustive but serve to show that if dis-peace is present, getting help to understand exactly what God says about these wonderful relationships is vital. The truth is, we all need to know where 'right' ends and 'wrong' begins. Then, as we deliberately choose to live God's righteous way – paying the price of peace – we find peace in our homes and families.

d. Dis-peace within

For many of us the place we experience greatest dis-peace is within ourselves, in our mind and inner world. Our mind, will and emotions are often referred to as our soul realm. We have always had a soul and its habit of worrying, being anxious, hiding personal fears and unrest stays with us after we become Christians. That is why a cool, calm 'Christian' exterior often hides a mind and heart in turmoil, unrest and anxiety.

Left unchecked, those internal stresses slowly destroy us. They stop us sleeping as our minds continue to whirl round with worrisome thoughts, they nibble away at our subconscious mind even while we are working, playing and worshipping. For us as Christians – the ones who now have peace with God – it makes us feel bad because we know we should be feeling peace! Are we therefore a lesser kind of Christian? Such thought patterns lead to condemnation and further dis-peace.

Is there an answer? Yes! Inner dis-peace can be dispelled by increasing God's government in your inner world. Your thoughts, inner choices and emotions – your soul – must be taken control of and brought under God's righteous rule. You must *take captive every thought to make it obedient to Christ' (2 Corinthians 10:5)*. This process is all part of being *'transformed by the renewing of your mind' (Romans 12:2)*, a transformation that takes the positional peace we have in Christ and makes it your inner, felt reality.

You see the peace we have in Christ is spiritual – it resides in our newly saved spirit realm which was previously dead.

Our task is now to work with God in a process that allows the fruit of the indwelling Holy Spirit – which includes peace – to pervade both our soul realm (mind, will and emotions) and our physical realm (bodily appetites). We must be led by the Holy Spirit; God in us:

> 'The mind of sinful man is death, but the mind controlled by the Spirit is life and **peace**' (Romans 8:6).

This is a large and very important part of us all. If it is one of particular concern to you, I recommend working it through with God by reading the companion study in this series called *Battle for The Mind* – it will change your life as it did mine.

Take control of your thoughts and inner world; it is the price of enduring mental and emotional peace.

e. Dis-peace in relationships

I'm sure that by now you know what is coming? Unrest in human relationships demands that we increase God's government there. So whether you are experiencing dis-peace in your church relationships, work relationships, the friends you do sport with or simply meet occasionally, find out what God says about handling those relationships and do it – that is the price of peace there.

Strangely, for Christians it is often relationships at Church that become the most problematic. Maybe it is because we are thrown together with such a random mixture of people but God knows best and uses those relationships to help us grow. For our part, we must increasingly handle those relationships in a godly way, confident that with increasing government comes increasing peace. So, for example, we have to do things God's way when it comes to:

- Our attitude to leaders in the church (Hebrew 13:17)

- The way we speak about each other (Ephesians 4:29)

- How we handle each other as teams of volunteers

- Our willingness to submit to one another's gifts and abilities (1 Peter 4:10-11)

- How we receive and give correction (Colossians 3:16)

- And sorting out any grievances God's way (Matthew 5:23-24, 18:15)

The way of wisdom

The Christian life is all about doing things God's way. But not in the sense of keeping a set of rules in the hope it will get us to heaven. We must never forget that our salvation is a gift from God and not earned or deserved by us in any way.

Knowing this makes us so grateful to God for his grace towards us, that we happily choose to do things his way. By doing so, we continue to do what is right, which leads to peace, joy and all the other fruit of living life with God. It is what the Old Testament describes as the 'way of Wisdom'. Proverbs describes Wisdom as being like a person who calls out to us to follow her example and choose to do right. As we do so it says:

'Her ways are pleasant ways, and **all her paths are peace'** *(Proverbs 3:17).*

All your paths can be peace if you will deliberately choose to walk in the way of Wisdom and increasingly do things God's right way.

That is the price of peace; a price that is always worth paying for the peace that follows.

'Of the increase of his government and peace there will be no end' (Isaiah 9:7).

Chapter 3
The Product of Peace

Why do you want peace?

I have found that many people who are working through anxieties, dis-peace and unrest want peace simply because they don't want the negative feelings associated with a lack of peace. 'I just want to be out of this unhappiness' is their heart-cry, so their pursuit of peace is driven by a negative root. But just wanting to be free from the pain is seldom a strong enough reason to fully pay the price of peace and consistently do things God's way.

The people who move to a settled place of doing life in peace by steadily increasing God's government in their lives – doing things his way – tend to hold on to it because they understand the bigger picture I am exploring with you in these studies. They have grasped that living in peace actually produces something very special in their lives. That becomes the pull, the attraction, the reason for ensuring they never again slip back into ungodliness and dis-peace.

The prize, that I am here calling the 'product of peace', is one worth paying the price of peace to hold on to – as you will see!

A man of peace

My point is best illustrated by the example of King Solomon. Solomon was a man of peace – in fact his name is derived from the Hebrew word meaning peace.

Solomon was the son of David, the greatest Old Testament king Israel ever had. He was the one described as being the 'man after God's heart' (Acts 13:22) and he became the benchmark by which all kings who came after him were assessed. It was a great achievement if a king 'followed completely the ways of his father David' (1 Kings 15:11, 2 Kings 22:2).

Even though David did great things, his reign was characterised by warfare rather than peace. He was a warrior, killing bears and lions with his bare hands as a youth (1 Samuel 17:34-35). He dealt with Goliath and the Philistine threat as a young man, then endured years of strife with Saul's household when he eventually succeeded him as king. The popular songs about David were all to do with his military exploits: 'David has killed his tens of thousands' (1 Samuel 18:7).

In the second part of his life David had to negotiate the stress of various attempts to depose him from the throne

– even from his own sons. Times of settled peace were few and far between in his lifetime for a whole range of reasons.

David was, of course, a great worshipper too. He re-established God's pattern for worship and set up what became known as the Tabernacle of David, a tent pending the building of a permanent structure as a centre of worship – the Temple.

His songs – 73 of our book of Psalms – still form the basis of worship for God's people today. But if you examine their content closely, many reflect his pain and difficulties, expressing commitment to God despite opposition and hardship. Fewer spring from a tranquil place of settled peace.

So, David's rule produced something very special but not the things that can only ever be produced in a time of peace. For that, a 'man of peace' needed to be on the throne, and this became Solomon's purpose in life. He illustrates for all time that **some things can only be produced in a time of peace** and it is that principle I want us to explore a little more here.

This is how David explained the situation to Solomon at the end of his life:

> 'David said to Solomon: "My son, I had it in my heart to build a house for the Name of the LORD my God. But this word of the LORD came to me: 'You have shed much blood and have fought many wars. You are not to build a house for my Name, because you have shed much blood on the earth in my sight. But you will have a son who will be a **man of peace** and rest, and I will

*give him rest from all his enemies on every side. His name will be Solomon, and **I will grant Israel peace and quiet during his reign**. He is the one who will build a house for my Name'" (1 Chronicles 22:7-10).*

So, in contrast to David's reign, Solomon's was to be characterised by peace and his mandate was to do things that can only be done well in a time of peace.

Peace produces

Peace produces things that times of war, conflict, stress, worry and fear can never achieve. Even Solomon, who had great wisdom and a gifted mind, would have focused on very different things in a time of conflict and stress rather than the things we discover peacetime produced in his life.

a. Personal fruitfulness

In the time of peace Solomon thrived as an individual. We read:

'He spoke three thousand proverbs and his songs numbered a thousand and five. He described plant life, from the cedar of Lebanon to the hyssop that grows out of walls. He also taught about animals and birds, reptiles and fish. Men of all nations came to listen to Solomon's wisdom, sent by all the kings of the world, who had heard of his wisdom' (1 Kings 4:32-34).

The time of peace allowed Solomon to think, explore, research and analyse the world around him and to document his findings. The range of animal and plant life encompassed by the verse above is staggering! No doubt the results of his research were the equivalent of modern encyclopaedias, the results of a lifetime of study and analysis.

Peacetime also allowed him to develop and express his latent musical and lyrical abilities – probably inherited from his songwriter father, David. Imagine the time required to write 1005 songs! No doubt our Bible book the 'Song of Solomon' was one of his best.

However, he is probably best known for his Proverbs, still one of the most popular books in our Bible. The reason is simple: Proverbs is a superbly insightful set of observations about human behaviour and contains the keys to living life successfully as one of God's people. How many times have we read one of the Proverbs and said to ourselves, 'that is spot on – life is just like that!' Have you ever wondered how long it took for those insightful proverbial maxims to be made? Each one is a classic and requires observation of life and human behaviour over time – they are a life's work.

My point here is simply that the time of peace produced a level of personal fruitfulness that a time of stress, conflict or warfare would not have allowed. The time of peace gave him the room needed to develop and release all his latent potential – and it is the same for us all.

This is why we need to live in increasing peace. Peace creates a context for our latent abilities to be developed to their maximum potential, which is what God wants. He wants you to be the best 'you' you can be!

Fruit frustrated

Sadly, if we live in stress, worry, fear and conflict, that potential never has the time or opportunity to be developed. As a result we bear less personal fruit than we could have and the knowledge of that becomes a very real burden for many Christians. They know they could have done more or produced more – but never did because of the chaos and stress in their lives.

Maybe you love art and have a gift for painting. You know it's there because when you paint you feel great and people always comment on how good your work is and encourage you to develop it. Deep down, you would love to paint more, or to even make a career out of it but you can never quite find the space to develop it. You were going to go to classes to hone up your technique … you dreamed of converting the spare room into a small studio … but it eludes you constantly because there is simply too much chaos in your life. Peace is rare. Money is tight because of bad spending decisions, relationships are tense in the home because of your short temper and you feel under constant pressure to be fixing the chaos rather than relaxing with a paintbrush!

Life goes on, characterised by the chaos and dis-peace, meanwhile deep on the inside regret about your unfulfilled dreams takes root. The older you get, the greater the regret becomes. Frustrated and disillusioned you may become bitter about you life and end up as one of those 'grumpy old people' we are all determined not to be when we are young and full of hope and aspiration.

Your personal fulfilment and fruitfulness is linked to having seasons of peace in which to thrive and develop your potential like Solomon did. So, I encourage you to get radical about the way you manage your life. Where there is dis-peace, deal with the reasons for it by working with God to increase his government there. Determine to do things his way, to pay the price of peace and thus experience increasing peace. Then, in the resulting times of peace and tranquillity, focus on developing your passions, interests and abilities. You will soon begin to enjoy the product of peace: personal fruitfulness at a whole new level.

b. Relational Fruitfulness

As we further explore Solomon's life we discover that he did not only thrive as an individual. Peacetime also had a major effect on his ability to develop and maximise his relationships, which benefited the whole nation.

The following passages describe the life God's people enjoyed during Solomon's reign:

> 'The people of Judah and Israel were as numerous as the sand on the seashore; they ate, they drank and they were happy' (1 Kings 4:20).

> 'During Solomon's lifetime Judah and Israel, from Dan to Beersheba, lived in safety, each man under his own vine and fig tree' (1 Kings 4:25).

They were thriving in the prevailing atmosphere of peace; they lacked nothing! A closer look shows that this was a result of the wider peaceful relationships they had with the nations around them, some of which Solomon also ruled:

> 'And Solomon ruled over all the kingdoms from the River to the land of the Philistines, as far as the border of Egypt. These countries brought tribute and were Solomon's subjects all his life' (1 Kings 4:21).

One relationship in particular, with Hiram King of Tyre (1 Kings 5), supplied vast quantities of timber and other raw materials in exchange for other goods because of their peace treaty. We also read of royal envoys, kings, queens and other nobility from across the world who visited Solomon and all brought gifts which contributed collectively to the prosperity of God's people. The Queen of Sheba is a notable example (1 Kings 10).

Solomon therefore resourced many nations and was in turn resourced by them. This was relational fruitfulness of a kind that only thrives in peacetime.

Resources are in your relationships

The nature of the Christian life is one of mutual interdependence. We need each other to thrive and reach our full potential. Only together do we represent God's House in the world today. Only together are we Christ's visible Body in action. Only together are we a community of faith in a godless world. Everything about our life and mission as the church requires us to work together for maximum results. I need you and you need me. Together we achieve more and truly express the multi-faceted amazing church Christ has commissioned us to build.

This truth demands we live and work in peace together because our resources are in our relationships. If we are stressed out with each other, or even at war with one another, we never enjoy the product of relational fruitfulness. If we are fearful of others we will avoid them. Or, if we are always defensive with people, they will soon get the message and stop approaching us. As a result, all the resources we could share and enjoy remain locked up within each individual, and that is a tragedy.

I believe this is why the Scriptures have such a strong emphasis on keeping the peace in all relationships. Peace creates a context for us to deepen our relationships and truly learn that our resources are in our relationships.

- If husband and wife are in constant tension and dis-peace, all they could enjoy together remains locked up.

- If team members never work to overcome their prejudices and misgivings about their co-workers, the fruitfulness of the team or ministry is impaired significantly.

- If a church is riddled with gossip, rumour and competitiveness, it will slowly die because we need peace to produce relational fruitfulness.

- If you have camped upon an old issue or offence and refuse to move on, you are robbing everyone of the wealth of experience, wisdom, practical help and blessing you could be.

Once you have understood that the product of peace is personal and relational fruitfulness - something we all want for a happy and fulfilled life - you will be more likely to pay the price of peace and do things God's way.

The product is worth the price! So make every effort to *'Seek peace and pursue it' (Psalm 34:14)* and to *'do what leads to peace and to mutual edification' (Romans 14:19).*

Chapter 4
The Purpose of Peace

We now come to a very important point in our exploration of living in increasing peace.

- The *price* of peace is clear: be willing to work with God in a process of increasing his righteous rule in your life. This leads to peace.

- The *product* of that peace is also clear: personal and relational fruitfulness, something we all want so that we can live a happy and fulfilled life to our full potential.

The question now becomes, for what purpose do we want peace? As we said earlier in these studies, peace is not an end in itself. God never granted peace to anyone just so they could indulge in it selfishly – however good it feels! Peace has a purpose.

God leads us into peace so that we can do things only achievable in times of peace. If we fail to realise this, peace can actually create some problems – which we will consider in due course.

What then is the purpose of peace?

A time to build

Let's return to our example of King Solomon. For him it was very specific; he had a task to fulfil in the time of peace, which was to build. God had said to David:

> 'You will have a son who will be a man of peace ... I will grant Israel peace and quiet during his reign. He is the one who will build a house for my Name' (1 Chronicles 22:9-10).

Solomon understood this, so when the time of peace arrived he knew what to do in it. He understood the purpose of peace:

> 'The LORD my God has given me rest on every side, and there is no adversary or disaster. **I intend, therefore, to build** a temple for the Name of the LORD my God, as the LORD told my father David' (1 Kings 5:4-5).

I would suggest that fundamentally, **peacetime is building time.**

In peacetime God expects us to get busy and build that which he has put us on the planet for. For each of us that will look different but in broad terms, the purpose of peace is to put the product of peace to work by building each area of your life. For example:

Family

Use the fruitfulness of peacetime to enrich and build your family. Spend quality time together, take on creative and adventurous projects, open your home, deepen your relationships and build a God centred family unit that becomes a purposeful tool in God's hand for the blessing of many.

Work

Apply the fruitfulness of peacetime to your world of work. Build your business creatively, apply yourself with skill and wisdom to your role in the workplace and develop your career. Build a work life that fulfils you personally and that blesses others too.

Self

The opportunity of peacetime has a personal application too: build yourself up. Build your skill set and knowledge base. Go to college or university, go for training, do that course you have always wanted to do. Build yourself up purposefully, always remembering that you are *'blessed to be a blessing' (Genesis 12:3).*

Church

Most importantly, emulate Solomon. His specific commission was to build God's House, the Temple, the modern equivalent of which is the Church.

Solomon built an awesome structure in which God was pleased to dwell, as represented by the Ark of the Covenant and the 'shekinah glory' that rested above it. However, that was only ever meant to be a shadow of the new covenant relationship we enjoy with God today as Christians. We are *'living stones' (1 Peter 2:5)* being *'built together into a dwelling in which God lives by his spirit (Ephesians 2:22).* God's glory is now shown to the world through his church (Ephesians 3:10) so our primary responsibility as God's people is to represent him well by building the Church.

Sadly many Christians today neglect God's House in favour of building their own lives; they have a modern equivalent of Israel's attitude immediately after the exile. Rather than building God's House, which was the primary task they had been given on returning from exile in Babylon, they became sidetracked and built their own homes instead. God said to them:

> *"'You expected much, but see, it turned out to be little. What you brought home, I blew away. Why?" declares the LORD Almighty. "Because of my house, which remains a ruin, while each of you is busy with his own house"' (Haggai 1:9).*

God points out a direct link between the time of peace they found themselves in and its purpose. He has freed them from exile for a purpose – to build the Temple as the centrepiece of the community that would then be rebuilt around it. God is always first and always at the centre. So he challenges them to:

"Give careful thought to your ways. Go up into the mountains and bring down timber and build the house, so that I may take pleasure in it and be honored," says the LORD' (Haggai 1:8).

The same provocation needs to be heard by many modern Christians who are easily sidetracked by the consumer driven materialistic society we live in today. We have peace and its product, but are we using that product to purposefully build God's House?

Not to do so leads to trouble! God is dishonoured, we remain unfulfilled and the world is left without a clear display of God's awesome community. If you, like me, believe that the Church is the most important organisation on the planet, you will prioritise building it where you live as the primary purpose of the wonderful peace you have in Christ.

Families, businesses, individuals and churches all thrive in times of peace, as long as they work hard to apply the fruitful product of peace.

Divine opportunity

The liberty and ability to build in a time of peace should not be underestimated.

Solomon observed that God had given him the opportunity to build by providing three things, which together created the conditions in which he could successfully build. He said:

'The LORD my God has given me rest on every side, and there is no adversary or disaster. I intend, therefore, to build a temple for the Name of the LORD my God' (1 Kings 5:4-5).

Like Solomon, you will also build most effectively when these same things are present:

a. Rest on every side

Every direction Solomon looked in, he saw peace. All his borders were secure and he had peace with the neighbouring nations. His family were in peace; there were no disputes, interpersonal tensions, or walking on eggshells in fear of upsetting someone. His staff were happy, his people content and he slept well at night.

He rightly attributed it to God. But as we have seen, peace comes through increasing righteousness. So if you look in some directions and still see dis-peace on the horizon – or even up close – increase God's government there, do things his way and before long you too will review your world and be able to say 'the Lord has given me rest on every side'. Then remember that those are the best possible building conditions, so get busy and build!

b. No adversary

When we are conscious that there is an adversary or enemy out there waiting to pounce, it takes some of our attention away from the building we are doing. Having one eye on the building and one eye on the horizon in case the adversary appears divides our attention. So to be able to say, 'there is no adversary' is a wonderful situation to find ourselves in.

For example, it is difficult to build *financially* if you are constantly aware of the adversary of debt or your tendency to make poor, impulsive spending decisions. That adversary needs to be defeated by concentrated effort and working a process with God. You need to develop a clear financial plan, a budget, and stick to it. That process itself is an expression of your desire to 'do right' and will eventually lead you to peace and the fruit it produces.

Similarly, it is difficult to build *relationally*, whether in a family, work or church context, if you are constantly aware of the adversary of past hurts, personal offence, or your failure to forgive people. The resultant enemy will forever prevent you purposefully building relationships and enjoying them to the full. Once again, this issue needs tackling by a focused process with God. As you do so, you will soon enjoy the joy of building deep purposeful relationships and the fruit they bring.

There are, of course, examples in the Bible and in life of people building whilst under opposition. It is possible to build in a time of conflict, but the things you build are different – they tend to be defensive things rather than life enriching things - and the speed and creativity of the building is always slow and low. But when we build in a time of peace, the building is exponential because there is no adversary to distract us.

c. No disaster

The third thing that Solomon says helped him build in peacetime was the absence of any disasters in his kingdom. He was not having to deal with famine, an outbreak of plague, the effects of an earthquake, damage from an unexpected weather phenomena like a storm, or a sudden building collapse, a personal tragedy, or similar.

Disastrous happenings always deflect us from our building focus. So we need to maximise the times when they are absent and live in such a way that keeps them at bay. I have observed there are two kinds of 'disaster' that we can encounter:

Controlled disasters: By this I mean disasters we have the ability to control by making good decisions in life, taking good precautions and preventative measures. The fact is, disaster often comes our way because of our own foolishness, poor choices or failure to plan. These kinds of disaster we can work with God to limit.

The choice to do things God's way, to use our common sense and to seek sound advice will always reduce the possibility of self-inflicted disaster. So if you find your ability to build is constantly restricted because your life lurches from one disaster to another, decide to do things God's way. Tackle the root issues. Get help. Do all you can to remove potential future disasters by exercising your power of self-control.

Uncontrolled disasters: By this I mean disasters you have no control over whatsoever. They just land in your life without warning. You did nothing to invite them into your world. Things like the sudden loss of a loved one, an accident, a freak weather incident, or changes in the economy that affect you adversely. When disasters like this appear, we must remember that God's grace is sufficient (2 Corinthians 12:9) and will help us to handle them without distracting massively from our building focus. Because they are not our fault, we can appropriate God's grace by faith and find strength, skill and wisdom to press through them. The righteous press through the storm and keep purposefully building!

Price worth paying

I hope that the more we explore this subject, the more you are realising that the price of peace is well worth paying.

- Doing things God's way is the *price*

- Personal and relational fruitfulness are the *product*, and,

- Building is the *purpose*

The purpose of peace is to build. So if you are in peace today, build for all you are worth and revel in this time of rest, without disasters or adversaries. What a wonderful way to build!

Chapter 5
The Problem of Peace

Peacetime is awesome! As we have discovered, it bears fruit in our lives and paves the way for us to build our lives on every front. It is a time we must hold on to and remain in. Doing so creates the context for the most fulfilling life possible.

In fact peace is so good, you would expect everyone to do all they can to hold on to it. However, peace does carry an inherent danger that we need to be aware of because, unless we are careful, it has the capacity to steal our peace! This is what I call the ***problem of peace***.

Feel-good factor

Peace feels good. It allows us to be creative and to productively build a purposeful life. But like all good things, too much of it can lead to us forgetting what it is actually there for.

Peacetime can make us lethargic, dull and self-indulgent. We can revel in peace and its benefits so deeply that we slowly forget its essential purpose and the price we need to keep paying to retain it.

At least a war keeps us focused and alert. We have a clear enemy to kill and issues to fight for, so are less likely to 'take our eye off the ball'. Having a clear sense of building purposefully in peacetime does the same for us – we have aims, targets, ambitions to realise and a sense of momentum. But if that slows down and we begin to over indulge in the benefits of peacetime for their own sake, danger is lurking.

A downward spiral

Once again, Solomon illustrates the 'problem of peace' for us very well. On the face of it he maximised the purpose of his peacetime by building God's House, his palace and many other civil engineering projects. His creativity exploded as we have described in the previous chapter. However, he sadly over indulged in some things during the time of peace and they created the problem I want us all to be aware of in this chapter.

Basically, he was distracted by some of the good things the time of peace brought into his world – including his wives and the complicated relationships linked to them. From his story we can observe a clear downward spiral into dis-peace, one we must learn from and commit to never following. You can read the full story in 1 Kings 11 where we see three clear steps:

a. His focus shifted

In this chapter we first see Solomon's focus begin to shift - very slightly at first but enough to start a chain reaction. He began to love the fruit of peace rather than the giver of peace. His riches and many wives became his first love. Without ever openly denying God, rebelling or doing anything seemingly bad, a shift took place in his heart away from the basis of his peace. We read:

> 'So Solomon … did not follow the Lord **completely**, as David his father had done' (1 Kings 11:6).

The word 'completely' says it all. He was still following God but not wholeheartedly like David his father had done.

All journeys back to dis-peace start with small omissions. We simply stop doing the good we know we should do. We forget that the price of peace has to be paid continually. The practical righteousness that leads to peace must be sustained; that's the price we pay. It was not a once for all time payment from our human perspective. I know that Jesus paid the price for our peace once for all time but our enjoyment of it means living his way, by faith, each and every day.

I wonder whether Solomon in his royal splendour had friends good enough to tell him when things began to slip? Or maybe they did and his pride got in the way? Or maybe his friends and courtiers were too afraid or felt it inappropriate to tell him in the first place. Whatever was the case, he made some poor choices that initiated the downward spiral.

The lesson for us must be that we all need great friends and relationships who will help us protect our peace. I want to be told if, in the good times of peace, I begin to drift away from God and I hope you do too. That's why the New Testament writers teach us to:

'Consider how we may spur one another on toward love and good deeds (Hebrews 10:24).

And we are to:

'Let the word of Christ dwell in you richly as you teach and admonish one another with all wisdom' (Colossians 3:16).

If my focus shifts, tell me and if yours shifts, I will tell you. That is what Christian friends do for each other because they genuinely want the best for each other; they want their friend to keep enjoying the wonderful product of peace.

b. He built the wrong things

Without the check and balance of good friends to keep him focussed, Solomon continued in his downward spiral. But at first glance you would be forgiven for not noticing. That is because Solomon continued to do what we are supposed to do in a time of peace - he built. The subtle shift came in what he built:

'On a hill east of Jerusalem, Solomon built a high place for Chemosh the detestable god of Moab, and for Molech the detestable god of the Ammonites. He did the same for all his foreign wives, who burned incense and offered sacrifices to their gods' (1 Kings 11:7-8).

In order to keep his foreign wives happy he built temples, idols and worship shrines for them to worship their false gods at. This was in direct opposition to God's law. The first of the Ten Commandments states *'You shall have no other god's before me' (Exodus 20:2)* and the second forbids idolatry of all kinds (Exodus 20:4).

So he was building, but completely the wrong things! If we are to retain our peace and the blessing that accompanies it, we must keep a careful eye on what we are building in the time of peace.

Building costs money, time and investment of life, so we only build what is close to our heart. We build what we love and we build for those we love. Show me where you are building in a time of peace and I will be able to see where your affections lie! Jesus made this point by saying: *'Where your treasure is, there your heart will be also' (Matthew 6:21).*

What are you doing with the fruit of your peace? Where is it invested? Is it all for you, for others, for God or what? All these are valid in their place, just be very careful not to build anything that is remotely unrighteous or contrary to God's will. To do so is to perpetuate a downward spiral towards what always follows unrighteousness – dis-peace.

c. His peace was disturbed

Having lost focus and built the wrong kind of things in peacetime, Solomon's peace was eventually disturbed. And it was God who did it!

In a previous lesson we observed that Solomon described the wonderful product of peace as being a time where there was *'no adversary'* to hinder him building. But that was about to change. The consequence of his downward spiral was that:

'Then the LORD raised up against Solomon an adversary, Hadad the Edomite, from the royal line of Edom' (1 Kings 11:14).

And it seems one was not enough because we then read:

'And God raised up against Solomon another adversary, Rezon son of Eliada ... Rezon was Israel's adversary as long as Solomon lived, adding to the trouble caused by Hadad ... Also, Jeroboam son of Nebat rebelled against the king' (1 Kings 11:23-26).

God is more committed to keeping us on track than we are sometimes! God wanted Solomon to be the man of peace, rooted in righteous, that he had called him to be. So to steer him back towards that wonderful place he disciplined him by sending these three adversaries. Ouch!

We must remember that we are God's children. Like all fathers, he loves us very much. He wants us to do right, find peace and enjoy its product. So when he sees us straying, he disciplines us like a wonderful father to get us back to the place of doing right and enjoying peace and its fruit again. Hebrews 12 explains this analogy in some detail and ends by saying:

'God disciplines us for our good, that we may share in his holiness. No discipline seems pleasant at the time,

but painful. Later on, however, it produces a harvest of righteousness and peace for those who have been trained by it' (Hebrews 12:10-11).

Notice what the discipline produces. **Righteousness** – because we are now choosing to do things God's way again – and as a result, ***peace!*** This whole process is designed by God to train us to do things his way by choice. We choose to embrace God's way – the price of peace – and once again enjoy its purposeful product.

d. Once bitten…

'Once bitten, twice shy' says the English proverb. The Bible carries many similar exhortations to allow the sharp pain of discipline to make us think again about straying from God's ways. The idea is that we are trained by it to live a life that lives for the most part in peace.

I'm sure, like me, you can identify with Solomon's downward spiral from the place of peace to dis-peace. The good news is that now you are aware of the problem of peace – that lingering temptation to shift our focus in the good times – you can be on your guard against it. One of the best ways is to have a great group of Christian friends and family around you, who can speak the truth in love to you should your focus ever shift.

Your peace was costly. It cost Jesus his life and it costs you the resolve of living Christ's way. So do not throw all that away by letting your guard drop. Stay focused; enjoy your peace to the full but never take it for granted.

Chapter 6
The Protection of Peace

Peace is precious! It is certainly worth paying the price for - of living a righteous life and doing things God's way. Also, I hope you now understand what an incredible opportunity peacetime offers you; a time to purposefully build with all the creativity, skill and wisdom God has given you.

For all the positive reasons we have explored in this book, it is important we say one last thing about peace and that is, we must know how to protect it once we have it.

Protecting your peace is not difficult or mysterious. In fact it involves much that we have already considered together. The difference is that the principles are now outworked purposefully for the protection of our peace, not to acquire it. This is all about holding on to the peace we have, valuing it highly and protecting it fiercely – for it is a most precious thing.

1. Do what leads to peace

Paul wrote to the Church in Rome and said:

'Let us therefore make every effort to do what leads to peace' (Romans 14:19).

In the context of these studies all I need to say is, remember what got you here. We have fully explored what 'leads to peace'. So, the first way to protect it is to simply keep doing what led you to peace in the first place. Keep doing right!

Reflect on how you achieved peace with God, came to peace within yourself, found peace in your family, work and relationships … and keep doing it.

Keep doing those right things, continuing to pay the price of peace.

Attitude is everything

As we all know, doing what leads to peace requires real effort at times and this is the emphasis Paul is making in the scripture above. The Apostle Peter made a similar point about the attitude we must have in our search for peace and then its protection:

*'For, "Whoever would love life and see good days must keep his tongue from evil and his lips from deceitful speech. He must turn from evil and do good; he must **seek peace and pursue it**. For the eyes of the Lord are on **the righteous** and his ears are attentive to their prayer"' (1 Peter 3:10-12).*

This passage makes it clear that doing right – keeping your tongue from evil and doing good – is synonymous with the pursuit of peace.

So both Paul and Peter inject the acquisition of peace with urgency and effort. One says *'make every effort'* the other *'seek it and pursue it'*. This attitude in particular is what protects our peace.

We protect our peace by continuing to do what leads to peace but with attitude! With effort, tenacity and eager searching. By doing so we are deliberately walking in the path of wisdom, and *'all her paths lead to peace (Proverbs 3:17)'*.

Radically righteous

At times we may need to be radically righteous in protection of our peace.

Seeking peace must never become a 'fudge' or a compromise. Seeking peace is never about lowering standards or behaviour to the lowest common denominator. Peace is never found by putting up with things that are wrong for a quiet life. The ultimate pursuit of peace will always demand a stand for righteousness and sometimes a radical one.

The word 'radical' has to do with roots; it describes the most fundamental or basic nature of a thing. So if something is radical, it goes right to its root, its essence. To be radically righteous therefore means being righteous to the root, the core, through and through. Sometimes the protection of our peace demands we stand for that kind of righteousness.

Phinehas, a young priest about whom we read in Numbers chapter 25, decided to be radically righteous to protect not just his personal peace but that of the whole nation. Israel was in trouble because of sinking moral standards and idolatry. As a result dis-peace and chaos were ravaging the nation. Adversaries were all around and sucking God's people deeper into unrighteousness. So he made a radical stand for righteousness by dealing not only with the enemy but also his fellow Israelites who were leading the nation into such chaos.

Because of his actions order was restored, peace returned and blessing followed. This is what God said about him:

'The LORD said to Moses, "Phinehas son of Eleazar, the son of Aaron, the priest, has turned my anger away from the Israelites. For he was as zealous as I am for my honour among them … Therefore tell him I am making my covenant of peace with him… because he was zealous for the honour of his God"' (Numbers 25:10-13).

Phinehas acted as God would have acted. He expressed radical righteousness and made a stand that restored peace to the nation. As a result, notice what his reward was - a **Covenant of Peace**. Righteousness always leads to peace!

This kind of radical righteousness is seen in the pioneers of history who stood resolutely for God's ways against the evils in society. People, for example, like William Wilberforce, who made a stand that culminated in the abolition of slavery. His modern equivalents are leading the stand against human trafficking, child poverty, abuse and the other evils in society. It may seem a million miles away from you in terms of scale. However, it is precisely the same radical righteousness that is expressed every time you decide to stand for God's right way in the face of the temptation to compromise, to be the voice of righteousness in the crowd or to stand against trends in modern society.

Peace is protected by resolutely pursuing righteousness. So keep doing what you know leads to peace.

Do what?

There will of course be times when you simply do not know what the right thing to do is. You know dis-peace and chaos exists in a situation, and you want to do the right thing and work towards peace. But exactly what that is, you aren't sure about.

In those situations always ask. God promises that: *'If any of you lacks wisdom, you should ask God, who gives generously to all without finding fault, and it will be given to you'* *(James 1:5)*. Basically, you are seeking peace by looking for answers from the Prince of Peace.

The Prince of Peace will speak to you through the indwelling Holy Spirit, who he has given to *'guide us into all truth'* *(John 16:13)*, and also through the Bible which is the written record of his will. That is why David wrote, *'Great peace have they who love your law, and nothing can make them stumble'* *(Psalm 119:165)*.

Also, ask the advice of your spiritual leaders, mentors or guides who have been walking with God longer than you or who know the Bible better than you do right now. Their breadth of experience will help guide you towards the peace you seek.

So, the first way we protect our peace is to keep doing what leads to it.

Use peace properly

The second way we protect our peace is by continuing to use it for the purpose it was given. Or putting it another way, by not abusing it!

God is the giver of peace. David wrote that '*the LORD blesses his people with peace*' *(Psalm 29:11)* and Jesus said '*Peace I leave with you; my peace I give you*' *(John 14:27)*. But as we have explained earlier in this book, peace is given for a purpose. That purpose is to build.

Use it or lose it

I have been in pastoral ministry for nearly 30 years as I write this. My experience of helping God's people find and live in the peace God has for them, plus the biblical principles we have explored in this book, have led me to a simple conclusion about peace: ***if you don't use it, you lose it, because you will abuse it!***

Not to use peace for its proper purpose is misuse by omission. Peace must be used, valued and protected for the awesome thing it is. But when it is misused or abused, it will go – as we have seen in our studies.

That was **Solomon**'s experience: He used peacetime to build the wrong things and as a result peace was lost.

It is also the pattern that characterises the time of the **Judges** in the Old Testament. Each Judge, the military and spiritual leader of God's people, led them back to God from a time of back-sliding and the resultant dis-peace. But every time peace was achieved through righteous living and doing things God's way again, they slowly slipped back into sin because they abused the time of peace; they used it to indulge themselves rather than build God's kingdom.

We also see this pattern in the church at **Laodicea**, which we read about in the book of Revelation. They had become rich and those riches were the fruits of peace – its product. But over time they had become dull and were now neither hot nor cold. They stopped building God's kingdom and slipped into self-indulgence and self-deception. To them Jesus said:

> 'You say, "I am rich; I have acquired wealth and do not need a thing." But you do not realise that you are wretched, pitiful, poor, blind and naked' (Revelation 3:17).

These examples and others in the Bible shout to me: *use your Peace properly!* In that way, you protect it.

Priorities

We have explored what peacetime should be used for in an earlier chapter and the breadth of things God loves us to build in partnership with him. But one Old Testament example stands out as a final illustration of this principle.

After the exile of God's people to Babylon they were commissioned to return to their land to do one thing – rebuild the Temple. The Temple was where God lived in that era. But today God lives in his people, the Church (see 1 Peter 2:5). So from this Old Testament incident we can draw a vital principle.

God's people had returned and started to rebuild the Temple – the purpose of their newfound peacetime – but they became distracted and stopped. And as we have observed before, they started to build other things like their own houses and businesses which were not the primary purpose for their peace at that time. So God sent the prophet Haggai to stir them back into action. He chastised them and urged them to *'Build my House so that I may take pleasure in it and be honoured' (Haggai 1:8).*

God also gave them a wonderful promise related to their willingness to build his House in the time of peace:

> *'The glory of this present house will be greater than the glory of the former house,' says the LORD Almighty. 'And **in this place I will grant peace**,' declares the LORD Almighty (Haggai 2:9).*

Building the Church is the most important thing we can build in peacetime. The Church is God's address in the world today, it is the expression of his life the unsaved first encounter, it is the agent of advance for God's kingdom in the world, it is the most important body of people on the planet! If we will prioritise building His House, God promises us that same peace.

No tin hats required

Your peace is not something you protect by building a defensive wall around it. Sometimes we convince ourselves that the Devil is out there coming to steal our peace, so we get our spiritual 'tin hats' on, dig in behind the wall and wait for him to attack.

This is not the kind of spiritual warfare required to protect your peace. Peace is protected by coming out from behind the wall and using peace time for its appointed purpose – whatever the apparent threat – and simply doing right. Get busy building things God's way and your peace will automatically be protected. James wrote:

> 'Submit yourselves to God. Resist the devil, and he will flee from you' (James 4:7).

Too often we have concentrated on 'resisting the devil' rather than 'submitting to God'. We must get this order right. First concentrate on submitting to God by doing things his way, which both leads to peace and protects your peace. Then, if the devil in one of his guises ever does appear on the horizon, resistance will be easy because you will be waging war from a place of absolute peace and security in God.

> 'You will keep in perfect peace him whose mind is steadfast, because he trusts in you' (Isaiah 26:3).

So, protecting your peace demands that you:

- keep doing what leads to peace and
- keep using your peace properly

3. Protected by peace

Finally, you must protect your peace because, when you do, your **peace will protect you!**

'The **peace of God**, *which transcends all understanding,* **will guard** *your hearts and your minds in Christ Jesus'* *(Philippians 4:7).*

Paul wrote this in a context of encouraging us not to be *'anxious about anything' (v5-6).* Worry and anxiety come from not knowing what lies ahead and the rapidly changing circumstances of life. There is no need to worry when peace is present because the presence of peace means we are doing things God's way.

When life gets difficult or unpredictable we can be tempted to deal with the emotional stress and anxiety we feel by changing things. But if deep in your heart you feel God's peace, even in the face of circumstantial turmoil and uncertainty, don't change a thing. Doing so can get you in a terrible mess! Instead, trust your peace. Let your peace protect you, staying confident that the presence of divine peace means you are doing things right and God will always bless and honour that.

Paul said it this way: *'Let the peace of Christ rule in your hearts' (Colossians 3:15 NIV).* The Amplified version of the whole verse says:

'Let the peace from Christ rule (act as umpire continually) in your hearts [deciding and settling with finality all questions that arise in your minds, **in that peaceful state**].*

Peace is the referee; it directs your heart and mind into God's right ways. In this way, peace protects us.

So, protect your peace because it will then protect you from going astray!

Conclusion

I hope that this short book has helped you understand and connect with the amazing peace we have in Christ. It is a most precious thing and vital to our success in the Christian life.

Remember, you *have* peace in Christ. It is yours as a free gift of his grace and no one can take that from you. But that positional peace must now become a felt-reality, expressed as an ever-increasing, all-pervading peace.

My prayer for you personally is that you willingly:

- Pay the **price of peace**
- Enjoy the **product of peace**
- Use peace for its true **purpose**
- Avoid the **problem** of peace and
- **Protect your peace** so that it can in turn, protect you

And for the Church or Christian community you are actively involved in building, I pray that you will enjoy the same fruit that peacetime brought to the early church:

'*Then the church throughout Judea, Galilee and Samaria **enjoyed a time of peace**. It was strengthened; and encouraged by the Holy Spirit, it grew in numbers, living in the fear of the Lord*' *(Acts 9:31).*

May it be said of you and your Church that '***of the increase of his government and peace there will be no end!***'